THE FISHERMAN AND THE CATCH:
CATCHING THE RIGHT WOMAN

RIC D. HARRIS

Outskirts Press, Inc.
Denver, Colorado

Outskirts Press, Inc.
http://www.outskirtspress.com

ISBN: 978-1-4327-4399-4

Library of Congress Control Number: 2009932026

Outskirts Press and the "OP" logo are trademarks belonging to Outskirts Press, Inc.

Author: Ric D. Harris

Editor: Zuzana Urbanek

PRINTED IN THE UNITED STATES OF AMERICA

Acknowledgements

Thanks to my lovely wife, my loving children, and my family and friends who have supported me. Thanks to my mother and grandmother, who have shown me the way, and to those I have learned from. Thanks to Detroit for giving me my background and the US Marines for giving me my structure. Thanks to the life experiences that have provided me wisdom and to the people who have made this book a reality. Most importantly, thanks to GOD for ALL!

Table of Contents

Introduction

This book is meant to entertain you. But it's also a fundamental guide to better yourself as a *fisherman*. While you will be amused, I hope, by the similarities of women and fish, you will quickly realize that the analogy is strong. Catching a good woman is much like going fishing on your favorite lake. This book will give you a deeper understanding about dealing with both fish and women. Don't be surprised if you actually decipher some mysteries about the behavior of women. At the very least, you'll become a better fisherman.

For years I have associated women with certain types of fish. I have observed the way women behave, the way they look, and how they choose men. And it dawned on me years ago that fish behave in the same way.

Friends ask me about how this works, since I have been married for over sixteen years (and today sixteen years is a long time), and I tell them how I went through many fish before I hooked my *bass*. I describe to my friends the difference in women, what they like, and how to catch them. When we all sit around just talking, I can see that what I describe really starts to sink in. It makes sense. It is both remarkably true and incredibly funny.

In recent years, as I became more active in church (which I must admit is one of the best fishing holes, if not *the* best). I would talk to some of the brothers in my Ministry about women and fishing (if we were close, and they knew that I meant no disrespect—you know how church folk can be sometimes). I would joke with the single brothers in the Ministry, using my hands as if I were casting, setting the hook, and reeling in the fish. These chats always provoked abundant laughter. Now, I want to share the laughter—and the significant insights—with you.

About the Author

Most people who write books are known for the work they have done, like bishops or pastors, civil rights activists, and so on; then there are those who maintain high-level political or corporate positions; finally there are sport figures, actors, scholars, doctors...the list goes on and on. All of them have taken the time to write books about what they know, what they have experienced, and the life they have led. So, I want you to know a little about the author of this book.

In my lifetime I have been called a playboy, player, and womanizer (I'm sure I have been called much more and worse). I also modeled, did comedy, and now run a successful business. People often look at a playboy or player as one who has game, one who snags women with ease, and one who has a different woman every day of the week. The important thing about *real* playboys and players—at least in my case and many cases—is that they don't hide it. Every woman I was with during that time of my life knew I kept company with other women. In some cases they knew each other. The misconception about playboys and players is that they misuse and abuse the women. That's far from the true woman-appreciating playboy or player—that's a *pimp*, and that's something I NEVER was called.

My wife often tells me I'm naïve about women because I never had to work hard to get one. She ought to know, after all. But she is right. It was not hard for me to get women; it was hard for me to keep them. Maybe that's because I kept them on the stringer and never took them home to filet. Or maybe I was not mature enough to maintain a relationship with one woman back then. Now I can sing a different tune, as I'm going on seventeen years of marriage, to a *sea bass* (what that means will become clear as you read on).

I remember the time I was referred to as a womanizer. My first thought was, "OK, and the issue is *what*?" A womanizer is a man who has short sexual relationships with many women.

Again I say, "OK, and the issue is *what*?" Back in the day we used to say, "Don't hate the player, hate the game" or "If being a player was easy, everybody would do it." I'm not bragging, just filling in the background. Pastors, preachers, and other men of the cloth always say, "A person who has never been addicted to anything cannot tell a person how to get off the addiction." Using that philosophy, one who has had many different kinds of women can tell you how to catch them. I wonder what the good "church people" will say about this book. I better put some scriptures in it to be safe. (All kidding aside, my church will get 10% from the sales of this book.)

Modeling was loads of fun. I worked in various shows around San Diego. As a matter of fact, I was the 1991 first runner-up for Mr. Black San Diego. Yeah, you go ahead and laugh, but listen to this while you are chuckling: in the '90s in San Diego—and I'm sure in any other city as well—there was an abundance of women around fashion shows and modeling contests. A *vast abundance of women*! Models, women who organized the shows, women who attended the shows. It was like fishing in a stocked lake on a fish farm.

Later I tried to be a comedian. In one of my routines, I used to talk about homeless people; you know, how they always walk around carrying their resume, "Will Work for Food." I remember once pulling my car over and yelling out the window.

"Will work for food? Well, hell, you got it easy."

The guy looked at me and said, "Got it easy?"

I said, "Yeah, I work for food, rent, and utility bills." I pulled off and yelled, "Don't forget cable and pay-per-view!"

I also used to talk about Babyface and that song "Soon as I Get Home." Now, this brother says he is a good lover, but he's going to buy her clothes, pay her rent, and cook her dinner when he gets home from work. If he's giving so much good loving, he would not have to buy the clothes and pay the rent. And that line about cooking dinner? I remember a time I actually came home from work—hungry and ready to eat—and being acutely aware that there was going to be trouble when I opened the door and heard that song, "Soon as I Get Home." There she was, my lady at the time, singing that song. "Honey," I said, "I'm home and I'm ready to eat." She looked at me and said, "You need to be like Babyface." I told her that if she looked like Pebbles, maybe I would. (Those of you that don't know Pebbles, Babyface's lady at that time, appreciate that she was *fine*.)

So, enough about my life. Just know that I do know women. During these earlier stages in my life, I had opportunities to study firsthand the many different types, flavors, and styles of women. I have known and dated women from every race and socioeconomic status, everyone from the girl in the hood to the corporate executive. And it all adds up to this: women really are like fish. So get ready to learn about the different types, what they do, what they like, and most importantly how to hook the right one for you.

The Fisherman and the Catch:

Catching the Right Woman

by Ric D. Harris

Fishing in the Beginning

Luke 5:9 states, "For he and all his companions were astonished at the catch of fish they had taken," and Jeremiah 16:16 states, "'But now I will send for many fishermen,' declares the LORD, 'and they will catch them. After that I will send for many hunters, and they will hunt them down on every mountain and hill and from the crevices of the rocks.'" Let's just say fish and fishermen have been around for a very, very long time.

There...now that I have cited these scriptures, maybe the good church folk will feel better and know that I have progressed in my walk, at least a little. At any rate, it should make them smile.

I began fishing about twenty years ago. When I started, it was just to see if I could catch a fish. You know what I mean, that "man against nature" thing. Going out to catch your meal and bringing it home to be cooked. Showing your woman that you can provide. That's how it was done when your grandfather was a child. Even when your grandfather's grandfather was a child, fishing was essential and gratifying, and it still is.

Fishing first intrigued me because a friend at the time talked about fishing as if it was the best-kept secret in the world. The first time he took me fishing, I caught nothing. That's because I went straight for bass. Everything I purchased for my rig was just for bass. I did not have anything in my tackle box to catch any other type of fish. I spent hours on the lake and brought back zip.

Now, before we set out that day, my friend had told me what to get. Of course, I did not listen. All day I watched him catch fish, while all I did was constantly untangle my line. He would just look over and chuckle. But I kept trying. When it was time to go home and he had a stringer full of fish, I thought to myself, "Sometimes you won't catch anything, but you can never give up."

Later I began to study the lakes I was going to fish, to find out what types of fish were in the lake and where they would congregate. I did research on the fish to see how to catch them. I got a new, bigger tackle box and filled it with different kinds of jigs, lures, test line, sinkers, and bobbers to catch all types of fish.

Is this not just like going after women? You find out where they hang out, what type of atmosphere they like, or what they like to do. It could be going to movies, seeing plays, dancing, or taking walks on the beach.

The next time I went freshwater fishing, I was not coming back without something on my stringer. It took time and patience to learn how to catch the fish. When I did, I mostly caught panfish (crappie, bluegill), trout, catfish, and bass. I caught other fish as well, like walleye and pike. But panfish, trout, catfish, and bass are my main choices in fresh water. In time, there was not a fish I could not catch in whatever lake I fished.

The Fisherman and the Catch

There were times I went fishing and told my wife not to cook—I was bringing home dinner. And I always brought dinner home, even if I did have to stop at the fish market on the way home.

Is this not just like looking for a woman? There are plenty of women out there and, as long as you don't give up, you will in time catch a few, even if you have to go to the fish market and buy them.

Over the years I have accumulated about ten fishing rods and reels. Now when I go out fishing, I have a rod rigged for every kind of fish that I like to catch. I even had a "poaching rod" at one time. This is the rod and rig you take when you go fishing on private lakes. It has to be something you don't mind losing because when the police are called or security comes, you either throw the rod in the lake, drop it and walk away (or run), or the police or security officer confiscates it. No matter, the rod is gone. You'll notice I said I HAD one of these.

Using a poaching rod is the equivalent of using a woman for a booty call. You know exactly what

I'm talking about. In booty calls, you do not want anyone to know who the woman is, you never take her out on a date where others can see you with her, and you only call her when you've been out fishing and did not get a bite. Poaching also applies to that situation when you roll over in the morning and say, "What in the ---- have I done," quickly grab your clothes, and run out door. Jamie Fox recorded a song about this: "Blame It on the Alcohol."

Types of Fish

The first thing you need to figure is what type of fish you want to catch. You can go after either freshwater or saltwater fish. Of course, there's nothing wrong with fishing for both; just understand that they are totally different. They vary in taste, look, smell, fight, and size. In each body of water (fresh or salt) are different kinds of fish. In most cases, freshwater fish will not survive in salt water, and vice-versa. You need to know where to look for the fish you want.

The Fisherman and the Catch

Dealing with women is similar. Each one has a certain element or atmosphere in which she is comfortable. For example, if a lady's comfort zone is a jazz club with a more mature clientele, she may not feel at ease among the younger crowd in a hip hop club. If a lady likes plays or operas, she may not like movies, but if she does want to rent a movie, it will be one with a plot, suspense, and a great climax rather than a shoot 'em up action movie. She's more into *The Color Purple*, *On Golden Pond*, or *The Secret Life of Bees* than *Judge Dredd*, *Rambo*, or *Fast and Furious*. It's like the difference between dressing semi-formal (suit and tie or blazer and slacks) to dressing in jeans that hang down to the knees, tennis shoes, and an oversized shirt that fits two or three people at the same time.

There are many freshwater venues, including ponds, lakes, streams, and rivers. Saltwater settings include seas and oceans. Fresh water has a low concentration of dissolved salt, whereas 1 kg of salt water has 35 grams of dissolved salt. You see how different each type of water is. Now associate this with women.

Freshwater women are those under forty. Most have not been through that many life experiences. They are still trying to find what they want, who they want, and how they are going attain both. In most cases, their bodies are firmer than those of women over forty...in *most* cases. These freshwater fish are your trout, catfish, panfish, and the most popular— bass.

Freshwater Fishing

Realizing that there are probably more people who fish in fresh water than salt water, and that most people are familiar with freshwater fish, let's start there. (Saltwater fish are covered in the next chapter.) This chapter focuses on freshwater fish, how women are similar to them, and how you can obtain the best catch in both realms.

Trout

Trout is exciting to catch and good to eat. However, you must have patience. Find yourself a comfortable spot because you may be sitting there for a while. You see, they can be difficult to catch because they are finicky. One reason is that the trout has limited vision, especially in murky or dark water. Due to this, its senses of smell, taste, and feel are intensified. This makes the trout very sensitive. As far as behavior, trout is one of those fish that will swim by itself, or it will swim with others. It travels to meet up with other trout in areas for spawning. Trout is very colorful, as you can see in the golden trout and the rainbow trout.

So, what kind of women are trout? These are the women who, in most cases, can go out alone but will meet up with friends at a club, restaurant, or coffee shop. They feel comfortable knowing others in the venue or being with a group, but they will go off on their own to explore the area. It's like when all the girls go out to a club and one or two break off from the group and walk around by themselves, only to come back later to let the other ladies know they are all right. They look good, they dress fashionably, and they have an open mind when it comes to life issues. They may not see what is coming, but they will catch it through one of their other senses. This means that a woman may not see you coming but will hear your BS a mile away. She will show some independence and not be afraid to step out on her own. She is a good catch and a thrill to be around.

Panfish

Panfish come in many types: you have crappie (white or black), bluegill, perch, sunfish, and even types of bass that fall under this category, like rock bass. This category of fish is called panfish because they are small enough to fit in a frying pan. Panfish travel in bunches or schools, which means that when you catch one, you will catch many. They are easy to pull out of the water, quick to clean, and very good to eat. The only problem I see with panfish is that you have to catch and eat a bunch to get full. Some may think it's worth it, while others may think it's a waste of time. Bottom line: when you catch panfish, you are not going to throw them back in the water.

Remember when you just started being interested in women? The mindset was, "There are many of them out there, and I just want whatever I can get." You were fishing for panfish. These are the young ladies who think they know it all. No one can explain to them how things are—since they can drive or can stay out past midnight, they know it all. They travel together for security and to have a sense of acceptance, which means they are easy to influence. There's always that one person or group as the leader, and others follow (if this concept is hazy, just go see any movie about high school or college students). These ladies make good practice because they will do what others do or say. They have not found themselves yet, and they write everything off to "just having fun."

Catfish

Catfish is one of those fish that is an acquired taste—not because they taste bad, but because of what they eat. Many people do not like catfish and will not eat it simply because catfish is known to be the bottom feeder in the lake. They will eat anything. Just think of the worst things that can be at the bottom of the lake, and most likely a catfish has eaten them. The smellier the bait, the better, to catch a catfish. Once I took some chicken guts and liver, I put some garlic on it, and I put the container outside for two days. It made great bait. I truly believe it's more of a psychological issue when people do not like catfish. I hear it all the time at home that what you put in your body is what will come out. Well, it's the same with catfish. If catfish eat junk, trash, waste, and so on, and you eat catfish, then in theory you eat junk, trash, waste, and so on. Catfish can be aggressive and territorial; however, they get along with each other. Catfish like a diverse habitat, including fallen rocks, submerged trees, old tires, and the like—kind of like the ghetto or the hood. Catfish put up a great fight and they are the most difficult to deal with. Be very careful with catfish, as they have spiny fins that they use as weapons. But don't get catfish twisted—just because they eat the smelliest and nastiest of baits, catfish surely taste good. If you are careful, they are well worth it.

I think LL Cool J said it best with "I need an around the way girl." He was talking about a catfish woman. You know, bamboo earrings at least two pair, a girl with a bad attitude, to get you in the mood when she talks with street slang. Have you ever been to a spot where every woman you see has burgundy or platinum hair? They smile and you see a gold tooth in the front or on the side. You might even see a front grill (the total upper or bottom teeth all gold). Each one is wearing earrings up and down the entire ear. You see a few nose rings and tongue piercings too. These women will have great figures, pretty faces, nice smiles (once you get past the gold teeth). And they will tell you off in a hot second. There is no telling where you will find these ladies, but one thing is for sure, they will be making noise and drawing attention, which will make them easy to find. At the end of the day, they make great companions if you can earn their respect.

Bass

The Fish

Bass is the best catch and has the best taste of freshwater fish. Going after bass takes skill, patience, knowledge, and experience. Bass have a complex and effective sensory system. They have traits of a predator, meaning that they will chase down and devour prey. They don't swim around an area looking for and hunting live bait. Rather, they sit back, covered and concealed, and when something they want gets in their view, they strike, inhaling it quickly. Some say bass are simple-minded, but I disagree because they are by far the hardest freshwater fish to catch. You have to work, and work hard, to catch bass. You have to know the water temperature in order to know if the bass will be near the top or on the bottom. You have to know how to work the bait and the kinds of bait to use. You have to know how to find bass because, unlike other fish, they don't swim in just any area of the water. Bass in fresh water come in six types; the most popular are the largemouth bass and the smallmouth bass. Both have special needs. For example, the largemouth bass is known to be a carnivorous predator, which means it will feed on other fish and crawfish and even frogs, snakes, bats, small birds, and—believe it or not—baby alligators. Bass is the kind of fish you have to work up to. If you go to the lake just to fish bass and don't catch any, you will go hungry.

Have you ever been in a place and had the most gorgeous woman walk in the room or stroll past you? When she does, you stop what you are doing, stop talking (and notice that every man and woman has also stopped and are all looking at her), and just say DAMN! That, my friends, is a bass. She is the one in the club that most men don't approach for fear of being turned down and having to walk away from her, knowing that everyone in the club is looking and laughing. She is the one that every other woman will look at and say, or at least think, "B----." She is the one that is dressed to kill from head to toe, hair and nails done perfectly, and has a sweet scent that makes you think of bliss when she walks past. When or if she looks at you and smiles, all you can do is smile back...and you are not sure she was smiling at you in the first place. She is the one that, a week later, you and your boys are still talking about, with your claim to fame being, "But she smiled at me." You can tell she's an independent woman because she purchases her own drink, pulls out her credit card to pay for the meal, and drives a high-end vehicle (Mercedes, Lexus, BMW). She is the one every man wants to be with but does not dare to talk to because he knows he will have to come at her in just the right way. It's not that she is "high maintenance" (which is what we men say when we know the woman is out of our league), but she has class, beauty, and poise. She has high standards and has set a high level of expectation. She will not substitute and will not waste time— so she does not give men time to work on it. If you are not ready, don't play with her. She can ruin you and break you down.

Now you know the types of freshwater fish, how to describe them, and what to look out for. To become a true fisherman, there is much more you need to know. The next chapter explains the saltwater (over forty) versions of these types. Then, in the next few chapters, I will take you through the required tools you will need to set the hook, reel in the fish, and get the fish in the boat.

Saltwater Fish

Over time, I got into saltwater fishing. I have always liked to eat grouper, red snapper, flounder, and whiting. Let me tell you, if you want to do this right, get a separate tackle box just for saltwater fishing. The fish you catch in salt water fight more and are a lot bigger. The jigs, rigs, test line, rods, reels, etc., are all different for saltwater fish.

My first time going saltwater fishing, I rented my rig on the boat that took us out in the ocean. I did this so that I could see what would be the best rig for me. When going saltwater fishing, it's best to use live bait (sardines or minnows). The minnows you use are so big that, once you put the hook across the bridge of the nose, you can just cast or drop the line in the water and feed the line (pull the line off the reel), and the bait will do the rest.

The Fisherman and the Catch

The great thing about fishing for grouper, red snapper, barracuda, and sea bass is that the rig, bait, and hook can be used for all these fish. That's why my saltwater tackle box is much smaller than my freshwater tackle box. I use a circle hook or a live bait hook, 15-lb test line, and a heavy fishing pole. The only thing that sometimes needs to change is the amount of weight on the line. If the fish swim toward the bottom, you need to add weight to the line to make it heavy enough to take the bait to the bottom of the body of water you are fishing. In my opinion, this simplicity makes saltwater fishing much easier than freshwater fishing.

There is another way in which it's easier to catch fish in salt water than in fresh water. You are on a boat, with a captain who knows exactly where to take you because of his experience and that big fish finder he has mounted in front of him.

On the other hand, it's also tougher to catch fish in salt water. This is because the fish are much bigger and stronger than those in fresh water.

I look at saltwater fish as I do women over forty. Think about it. Bigger and stronger—don't think big in size; think big in ideals. For the most part, they have their life in order, they are career- and goal-oriented, and they have had many life experiences. When you think of strong, think of their maturity, knowing how to handle situations head on, dealing with adversity, and being someone who will be by your side when things get tough. (Please do not mistake her for someone who will just let you sit on the couch and watch TV while she goes off to work.) Also think strong as in being direct and not beating around the bush, no matter what the cost.

When I was younger, the idea of a Sugar Daddy was often talked about. For those of you that do not know, a Sugar Daddy is an older man who takes care of a much younger woman financially, while the woman takes care of him romantically.

Now, we have the Cougar. My wife told me about this term. A Cougar is an older woman with a younger man. Two examples that most people are familiar with are Demi Moore and Ashton Kutcher (sixteen years younger) or Mariah Carey and Nick Cannon (eleven years younger). What the woman (a.k.a. the Cougar) offers the younger man could be financially or otherwise helping the young man in times of need, and mostly what the Cougar wants is a feeling of youth and intimacy. Most of these women have children and have raised their boys to be men. They are looking for a relationship—intimacy with someone who makes them feel young—they are NOT looking for another boy to raise!

I remember a time when I went saltwater fishing. The boat pulled into an area, and we caught our bait. The deckhands pulled the bait off the line and put it in a bait tank. Once we had enough, we moved on. There were five of us fishing, but at the end of the day, we caught 142 lbs of fish. We caught amberjack, trigger fish, grouper, and red snapper. Talk about a fight! In most cases, we fought for about twenty minutes to reel each fish into the boat. Some of us had on a harness to put the rod in, to help reel in the fish. I did not. I had to put the end of the rod into my hip as I pulled up on the rod when reeling in. When it was all over, the end of the pole had scraped my skin away. But the fight was well worth it. Just like women over forty years old: they put up a fight because they have experience and they do not have time for games. So the fight is more mental, philosophical, and rational. They can sometimes be easy to catch because, at a certain age, everyone gets lonely, everyone feels as though they have lost it, and they get self conscious about their looks changing. But believe me when I say that these women are well worth it. So, when I think of women over forty, they remind me of grouper, barracuda, red snapper, and sea bass.

The first time I was with a woman older than me, I thought that she was going to be old in her ways. I was going to summer school and she was a teacher. Not only did she teach me things, but when I got it wrong she made me do it all over again! Don't assume or be quick to conclude that these women are all old in their ways or salty, down on everything, or depressing. In the Marine Corps we used the term "salty dog" to mean an old timer, a Marine who has years under his belt, a Marine set in his ways, kind of like a Gunny Tom Highway. Go rent *Heartbreak Ridge* and you will see what I'm talking about. And "Oorah" to my fellow Marines! Semper Fi, Devil Dogs!

OK, I'm back.

When it comes to women over forty, salt takes on another meaning—this lady is the salt of the earth, someone who will be there for you when times are hard, someone who can help or advise you because she may have been through it herself, someone who will be true to you, and someone who will support you. In most cases, she will support you—but as I stated before and will again, these women are not for games. These women are like fine wine: the older the wine, the better the taste! Now you see why so many younger men are with older women.

Grouper

Red Snapper

Barracuda

Sea Bass

The saltwater fish types of women are basically more mature versions of the freshwater fish. This table shows how it works.

Freshwater Fish	Saltwater Fish	Characteristics
Trout	Grouper	• independent but likes to be with friends • looks good, dresses fashionably • has an open mind • sensitive to your BS • thrill to be around
Panfish	Red Snapper	• hangs with her friends for security • thinks she knows it all, but follows the leader • suggestible • just wants to have fun
Catfish	Barracuda	• girl from the hood • good looking and knows it • will tell you off in a hot second • makes noise and draws attention • a great companion if she respects you
Bass	Sea Bass	• most beautiful woman in any room • has class, beauty, and poise • holds high standards and high expectations • does not waste time or give men time to work on it • not to be played with, she can ruin you

The Fisherman and the Catch

These women compared with saltwater fish have the same traits as their freshwater counterparts; it's just that they have matured and gotten wiser, smarter, tougher, stronger and more ambitious, creative, determined, elegant, inventive, stylish, and strong-mined. And even sexier.

There is no special line a man can use to catch her. Just know that whatever line you do use, the line needs to be tough enough to hold her, and your fishing pole needs to be strong enough to reel her in. You'd better be honest with her from the start, and that is if she asks you questions. Nine times out of ten, she is not going to ask you much of anything because she does not want to answer *your* questions. She is secure being by herself until the time comes when she wants to be bothered or she wants companionship. That's one thing that makes women over forty easier to catch. It's not that they are easy—it is that they know what they want and won't waste time in going after it.

Here are some examples of the difference in the freshwater women and their saltwater equivalents:

- A young woman who is a trout will listen as you're trying to impress her by, say, letting her overhear your conversation, or will wait if you tell her to wait until you get back.

- A mature woman who is grouper will say, "Excuse me, you need to take your call somewhere else," or she'll walk away. If you tell a grouper to wait until you get back, she will say, "Find me when you are done."

- A young woman who is a catfish will hint, "My electricity (or cell phone, or whatever) will be turned off if I don't get help." She'll tell you she is struggling.

- When she gets older and becomes a barracuda, she will just say, "Give me $____ so I can pay my bills." If she is struggling, she will say, "You need to help me."

- A young woman who is a panfish will let you be intimate with everyone in her group, just because she likes you and heard you are good in bed, while all the time telling herself it's just her you are sleeping with.

- A red snapper will justify in her mind why it's OK for her to be sleeping with you even though you are seeing other women.

For bass and sea bass, there is no example. She is always classy and pulled together. After forty, she's just that much wiser.

As I describe how to make the catch for each type of fish, I'll refer to the freshwater variety. The same applies in each case for the corresponding saltwater fish...and the women each one represents.

The Fisherman

As a fisherman, you should know what type of fish you want to catch. There are those fishermen that will only fish for one type of fish. Perhaps they are used to the mannerisms of the fish, they like the way the fish tastes, and they like the fight the fish puts up. Or, it could be simply because they do not know how to catch other types of fish. These are the fishermen you see walking around with one fishing rod and a small tackle box.

On the other hand you have the fisherman who will try to catch everything in the lake. He has several fishing rods, and each one is rigged a different way to catch specific types of fish. His tackle box is the size of a small suitcase.

It's the same with going after a woman. You first must know what type of women you like in order to make the right catch. Most men think, "I'll just go out there and get a woman," with hopes of changing the women they meet to suit them. Listen to me: YOU CANNOT CHANGE A REAL WOMAN. It's like trying to catch a trout with a plastic worm. It's just not going to happen. Now, if you take off the plastic worm and put on a real worm, you may catch that trout.

So the questions to ask yourself are these: "What kind of woman do I like? And where do I find her?" One easy way to answer these questions is to figure out what *you* like first. Go to places where *you* have interest. If you like music, go to places that play what you like, be it jazz, reggae, hip hop, R&B, country western, oldies, or whatever. If you like to dance, go to places that feature your kind of dancing, whether it's swing, stepping, ballroom (Detroit style), or bump and grind. If you are into art exhibits, museums, or church (which, as I said, is a great fishing hole), go where you have interest because that's where you will find the woman that has a similar interest.

This is known as identifying your fishing hole. In becoming a fisherman, know what you want and set up your rig accordingly. In the case of women, put yourself in an environment in which you will be relaxed and able to strike up a conversation with a lady. If you are uncomfortable, you will be nervous, and nervousness sets off perspiration and an actual odor of fear. Fish can sense humans by their odor. Women have a similar sense.

Have you ever been in a club, lounge, or bar and noticed that brother just leaning on the wall, not talking to anyone? It's probably because someone told him that club was a good spot to go fishing. The thing is, maybe it was, but just for the person that told him it was a good spot. As a fisherman, you have to find your lake and your own fishing hole.

Men by nature need women to show them compassion and give them intimacy. Women are similar. They need a man to show interest in what they think and do, affection (not just sex; it could be as simple as a backrub or snuggling while watching a movie), attention to their details (how they keep the house or make a good meal), and finally praise for all they do. Both men and women need to feel respected by one another.

Respecting women (and the nature of different women) will also include deciding which women you should be fishing. For example, when I used to model, I was not fishing for bass. I went for panfish, catfish, and occasionally trout. I knew I was not ready to settle down. I was having too much fun. The times when I felt I could handle a commitment, I fished for trout. But it never worked out...there were just so many panfish and catfish in the water.

As I matured, I fished for bass. I will be the first to admit that, as I was reeling them in, my line snapped and I lost the fish. There were also times when I thought she was my bass, only to find out she was a catfish.

Often we men think there is something better for us on the other side of the lake. We may have a good woman and think there is someone better out there. So we start putting more lines in the water. There is nothing wrong with fishing for other or different types of fish at the same time (remember, I have a pole rigged for all kinds of fish when I go fishing), just like there is nothing wrong with seeing several woman at the same time. The problem arises when you do not respect yourself or the women enough to let them know up front what you're doing. Let's face it: some men and women do not want a commitment. If that is where you are in life, let it be known from the start. And if that's the case, you might want to stick with panfish and catfish or red snapper and barracuda.

Rig Up

As mentioned, the rig or setup is different for every type of fish. Rig simply refers to the fishing rod, casting device (reel), test line, and bait (live, plastic, or lures). Yes, it's true: each type fish requires a different rig. You will not be able to catch a trout using a rig for bass.

What's in the Rig?

- The **fishing rod** can be light, medium, or heavy. This indicates the flex and strength of the fishing rod. It can be made of any of a number of materials, and each rod is created to go with specific conditions: the fish you want to catch, the line and bait

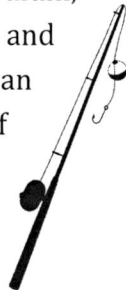

you'll be using, even the water and wind conditions.

- **Reels** come in either spinning or bait casting. You can use both for all types of fish. However, each one is designed for a specific type of fish and the bait that you will be using.

- The level of **test line** (fishing line) is simply the strength of the line, as different strengths are needed to catch different fish. Test line can be as low as 1-lb test line and go as high as 100-lb test line.

- Next, you have to decide what size **hook** you will use. Hooks come in various styles, shapes, and sizes. Some hooks are designed specifically for different types of bait. There are hooks for live bait and plastic bait. Sizes vary from a 32 to a 19/0. When dealing with hooks, the larger number indicates the smallest hook size. I won't go into the minutiae here—there are plenty of guides that describe how the sizing works.

- Finally, you need to decide what type of **bait** you will use. This point has stumped many fishermen. Plain and simple, you will either go with live bait (and then need to choose which type) or some kind of manmade plastic bait like lures, flies, poppers, spoons, crank baits, and jigs. It all depends on what you are fishing for.

The Rod

What type of fishing rod should you use? The type of fishing rod varies for the type of fish you want to catch.

Light rods provide for quick moves, and they have an extremely noticeable bend when you get a strike from a fish. They are very thin and really not much to work with, but they can be used by beginning fisherman or for smaller fish.

The Fisherman and the Catch

Medium rods are a step higher. The feel is good, but, depending on what you are fishing for, you have to watch the line because the bend in the rod is not as oblivious as in a light rod.

You can use a heavy rod to catch whatever is in the lake. The bend will be noticeable when you get a nice strike from a bigger fish. When you set the hook (we will talk more about this later), you will easily see the bend. The great thing about medium and heavy rods is that you do not have to worry about catching a fighter and having it snap your rod.

Don't think for one moment that the fishing rod you have (keep it clean) will not make a difference in the type of woman you can catch. The fishing rod is what you need to hold that woman. So, let's see what type of fishing rod you have.

Fishing Rod Quiz

1. Are you working?

2. Do you just have a job, or do you have a career?

3. Does your paycheck barely pay the bills, or does it put some money in your pocket?

4. Are you living paycheck to paycheck?

5. Do you own a home, or are you renting?

6. Do you live alone, do you have roommates, or are you still at home with your mother, saying, "I still live at home because it's free"?

7. If you are living with mom, ARE YOU PAYING YOUR MOTHER SOMETHING FOR LIVING IN HER HOUSE?

8. Is the area where you live safe? Is the neighborhood clean?

9. Whether it's a house, apartment, or your mother's basement, is your living space clean?

10. Are you paying your bills on time?

11. What are you driving?

12. Do you have a high-end car, something nice, or a hoopdie? (You know what a hoopdie is…something moving on four wheels that leaves oil stains in the driveway, with windows that don't roll up or down, rust on the body, and smoke coming out the exhaust.)

13. Are you walking or taking the bus?

14. Do you have clothes or outfits for different occasion? (You know what I mean…do you go out, go to work, and go to church in the same outfit?)

I can go on and on, but by now you should have the picture. Don't get me wrong, these questions are not to say who is better than someone else. After all, you can live in a bad area, drive a hoopdie, and have a job that just pays the bills, and still catch a nice fish. Oh, I mean a nice woman. But face it: your lifestyle has much to do with your prospects in a relationship.

What you are holding will make a difference in the type of fish you will catch...and in the women you can attract. Always remember this—it's up to you, the fisherman, to decide what type of fish you want to catch. If you are going to catch a bass, you won't do it with a light rod, or perhaps even a medium one. So, when you are ready to go from a light fishing rod to a medium and then to a heavy, all you have to do is *change* what you are doing, knowing that change comes with hard work, pains, strains, and then gains. This is true in life as well as in holding on to a woman.

Test Line

Test line is the element of your rig that is essential to reel in the fish. It's what you tie the hook onto, cast into the water, and pull on using the rod. Choosing the right test line is very important to successfully catching a fish or even getting a bite.

The numbers on a package of the test line identify the diameter of the line as well as the tested pounds of force the line can take before snapping (e.g., 2-lb test line can break beyond two pounds of force). It stands to reason that you would not use a 2-lb test line to catch a 15-lb catfish. But you can use a 2-lb line to catch panfish or trout. Test line comes in different materials: nylon monofilament, braided, fusion, and fluorocarbon, all of which come in different colors and levels of stiffness. Each type of line has its own sensitivity level and shock level. Shock level is the reaction in the line when the fish strikes the hook. When deciding on the type of test line, make sure you know the type of fish you want to catch, as the line you choose needs to be strong enough to keep the fish on the hook.

When I was growing up, I used to watch movies to gather lines for picking up women. My favorite line that I made into a pickup came from *Lady Sings the Blues*, when Billy Dee Williams looked up at Diana Ross and said, "You want my arm to fall off?" I have used that line as motivation to develop new lines. Let me tell you, it worked...at least back then.

Back in the day, I used to go to jazz spots in San Diego. One of my favorites was Humphrey's by the Bay. This place was known to be frequented by professional business women. They would sit at the bar or around the piano, moving their heads from to the beat of the music. This was the period when the jazz band Fatburger was playing there on Sunday nights. One night, I spotted a lady sitting at the bar drinking Cognac. I walked over and ordered a Jack and Coke (my drink back then), then looked at her drink and said to the bartender, "Another Cognac for the lady." Before the bartender walked away, I asked him to wait, and looked at the lady. "Is it OK for me to get you another drink?" She did not say a word, just grinned and nodded her head. Of course, I did not know where she was coming from because she hadn't spoken. After the bartender brought the drinks over, I picked up her drink, bent over to her, and whispered in her ear, "You want my heart or just my soul?" She looked at me and said, "Whichever one you want to give me, and I will work on the other." Her comeback line was just as good as my pickup line.

The Fisherman and the Catch

Your test line is what you say to her when you first see her. It matters what you say and how you say it. Are you speaking clearly so you can be heard? Are you using good grammar? And how's your timing? In deciding when to speak, timing is everything, as this will be your initial conversation. Your entire approach is part of your test line, including the way you walk toward her, your swagger, the eye contact you make, the nod, the wink, the smile or grin you acknowledge her with—it is all vital.

Trout

To catch trout, I usually use a 3-lb test line, sometimes a 2-lb line. Many fishermen use a 4-lb to 6-lb test line. It all depends on your skill, how you let the fish run, and whether you don't want to lose what you catch. I have even used an 8-lb test line with a 3-lb leader. All this means is that I had 8-lb test line on my spin cast reel and connected it to a swivel with 3-lb test line tied to the other end. It's important that what the fish sees is inconspicuous. You see, the heavier the test line you use for trout, the easier it is for them to see it and go to the next fisherman.

What this is saying is that the line needed to catch this type of woman is not heavy—in other words, don't BS her. Believe me, she will see right through it. She knows when someone is handing her a bunch of nonsense. Keep in mind that this type of woman moves around, so she is quick to move on. So, to catch one, you have to be upfront right from the beginning. I'm not saying you should tell her your life story, but be real. Don't name-drop, talk about all the money or toys you have, or try to impress her. You know what I'm talking about— going up to a lady with your keys in your hand so she can see the Cadillac key chain, or acting like you are talking on the phone while letting her overhear your conversation as you drop names. She will not be impressed. You actually don't need to try that hard. She is not looking for all the frills and thrills. She is looking for a good man and someone that is going to be honest and straightforward.

Panfish

Probably the easiest freshwater fish to catch is panfish. You can use test line anywhere from 2 to 8 lb. Remember what I stated before—once you catch one, you can catch many because they are all together. Get yourself a light fishing rod and go to work.

Back in the day, people used to catch panfish with a cane rod and a bobber. When that bobber went under water you knew you had a fish. Panfish is great for the beginner. It's the fish you let the children go for because a child's attention span is short. As a beginning fisherman, I would suggest targeting this fish to learn how the bite feels, especially if your attention span has not yet matured.

The ladies that are associated with panfish could be referred to as "groupies." Remember when you were somewhere between sixteen and twenty-one, and you played football, basketball or baseball in high school or college? Groups of young women followed you around, wanting to know you or help you with your homework. Even if you didn't play sports in school, don't think for one moment that panfish are not your catch. These could be the young ladies that were in your chess club or glee club or on the debate team. These are the ladies in sororities, social clubs, or just hanging out together. All you had to do was get one, and the others wanted you as well. Even into their mid twenties, these women often travel together, so they all know every male friend or boyfriend. And what happens next? She tells her girlfriends how good you were, or how nice you are, and now the girlfriends want to get with you just to see if she was telling the truth. When it is all said and done, you've got them all. You know none of them can keep a secret.

The Fisherman and the Catch

In high school I played football and ran track. It did not take much to catch this type of young lady. The great thing was that, when you got one, you got some—if not all—of her friends. It's the same in college—if you ever joined a fraternity or even went to a frat party, you know what I'm talking about. If not, just watch old episodes of *Beverly Hills, 90210* or *Melrose Place* and watch how Dillon (*90210*) or Jake (*Melrose Place*) got the ladies.

The line you use for these ladies is just showing some interest in them. Remember that panfish are easy to hook, so the lightest test line will catch you one. Take them out, carry their books, and give them cards or flowers just because. Tell them how cute they are, and how well they dress. You'll soon hear their friends talking about you and saying things like, "Why couldn't (so and so) be more like (fill in your name)?" No disrespect to the ladies, but they just have not matured enough to be less interested in someone else's good thing. But I will say this: panfish are sweet, and so are these ladies. Not a bad catch at all.

Catfish

Remember that catfish are good to eat, but a lot of people and cultures don't mess with them because they are hard to deal with and they are known to be the bottom feeders. Catching catfish is not difficult, but they can grow to be the biggest fish in fresh water by far. I have used 12-lb and 15-lb test line and had my line snap. Some fishermen have been known to use 20-, 40-, or even 50-lb test line. It makes a difference, as catfish can grow to weigh over 100 pounds. And they put up a fight. You will need heavy test line if you want to reel them in. One important thing about catfish: they will run for cover. After you sense a strike at the bait and pull up to set the hook, the catfish begins its fight by swimming for its hole or under something in the water to prevent being reeled in.

Tell me this is not the "Around the Way Girl." Do you know how much drama there is in dealing with a girl from the hood? Hell, you will need all the line you can get. You may not need strength

The Woman

when trying to talk to her, but you sure will when putting up with the neighborhood and those who live in that hood (or, should I say, projects), the baby daddy drama, and just wondering if you are safe. This reminds me of those women hanging out at 45 Park (in San Diego) where we used to shoot ball. The park would be full of strapless shirts, hot pants, burgundy hair fried and laid to the side, and a ton of gold. These women are a lot of fun, but to get to the fun, you have to let them know you are not scared. You have to let them know you can go to their environment and not worry about the small stuff. These women are used to being pulled hard, like a catfish hooked with a 20-, 40-, or 50-lb test line. So, your line needs to show strength, your attitude needs to show confidence, and your demeanor needs to show that you are not afraid. Once a man has built up his strength and confidence when dealing with women, he can succeed in life. At least he will not be afraid to take on a challenge.

Chapter 4

Bass

The Fish

Where do I begin with bass? This is by far the smartest fish in the lake. The test line you will use to catch bass varies because you have largemouth and smallmouth bass. You can use 6- to 8-lb test line, if you *think* you are skilled enough to do so. Some fishermen use 8- to 12-lb line for both largemouth and smallmouth. I have seen fishermen use 15- to 25-lb test line for largemouth. The professionals, the ones you see on TV in the Bass Pro Tournaments, use 12- to 18-lb test line. One might wonder why professionals don't use a lighter test line to show their skills, and I'll tell you why: MONEY! They do not want to lose a catch during the tournament. Using 8-lb test line or lighter increases the chance of getting your line snapped. This is when you need to have a good technique and know how to play with the fish. Sometimes you may have to let the fish run to tire them out or get untangled from debris. You also need the finesse to guide them as you are reeling them in.

The Fisherman and the Catch

This type of woman is truly the best catch by far. Many ladies may think of themselves as a bass, but on reflection they are really a trout or a nice-size panfish. Due to the way this lady carries herself, it is hard to say which line to use. Those who have tried know that she may see the line a mile away and just walk away from you. It takes time to catch her, and it will probably not be a first-time, first-sight event. If you are expecting that, you need to go fishing for catfish.

You may think you are choosing her—if that is what you are thinking, move on to trout because you will not catch the bass. In truth, she is choosing you. Just like the bass fish, she will ease up to your line and then may just walk away, leaving you doubting yourself and sending you back to panfish. It's not just a great line that will pique this woman's interest; it's the whole package. You have to make yourself appealing to her but not flamboyant. Your look has to be tight (hair, wardrobe, cologne, the way you walk, what you say, and how you speak). Your line needs to be one of buoyancy and assurance but not arrogance. Your compliments must be sincere but not seem desperate. She is a great catch—the one that you can take home to mother. She is the one that you can stay married to for seventeen years and look forward to years to come.

Hook and Reel

Everyone knows you need a fishing hook to catch a fish. The hook is tied to the end of the test line before you cast. Hooks are also used to hold the bait that attracts the fish. When the fish strikes the bait, the hook is set (pulled up in the mouth of the fish), allowing the fisherman to reel in the fish.

So far we have talked about the fishing rods you will need to catch various kinds of fish. The fishing rod is where it all begins; you need the rod to hold the test line. Test line is the strength that holds the fish. If you use the wrong size test line, either the fish will see it and not come near you or will snap the line because it is not strong enough to hold them when they begin to fight. And all fish put up some level of fighting.

The hook is the final piece of essential equipment in the rig. The reel can be a part of the rig, so it's included here. However, I have fished without a reel, and there are reel-less poles made for various types of fishing.

But you always need a hook.

How does one hook a lady? What does it mean to have her hooked? Well, you hook her by having a good rod and test line. Having her hooked means simply that you have her at a point where she is truly interested in further communication with you after the initial contact. Once she is hooked, your objective becomes to reel her in.

When you are fishing and the fish strikes your bait, the hooking process and reeling in process happen simultaneously. When you set the hook, you are pulling up and reeling in the fish at the same time.

Reeling in a lady is the same. You set the hook by keeping her interested in you long enough to develop a relationship or to achieve whatever you set out to do. You begin to reel her in through further communication and moving into the dating phase. Dating allows both of you time to see if you are compatible or right for each other. During this time, she can still snap your line, and you will lose her. Of course, this depends on the type of man you are and what type of woman she is. During this phase, you will discern whether she wants to continue to see you. You will be able to tell by how the dates progress, how comfortable you are with each other, how effectively you both communicate, and how often you want to communicate. You will know that the reeling in is going well when you see that your time with her is becoming more frequent and your communication is enhanced.

Now, don't be confused or misled that a span of time is a factor in hooking her and reeling her in. I'm sure I'm not the only one who has cast a line, set the hook, reeled her in, and took her home to filet all in the same night or within a few days. But then, that was my objective as a fisherman back then.

Trout

The best hooks to use for trout are small hooks and small treble hooks (the ones with three hooks in one). The smaller the better because trout will swallow the hook and bait, and it has to be small enough for them to do just that. I have pulled in trout and found the hook was in their stomach. A #8 or #10 hook works well.

With these women, as I stated, you have to be patient. It's not about impressing them. It's all about showing them that you are a genuinely good man. What's wrong with meeting a lady, extending your hand, and saying,

"My name is ----. It's a pleasure meeting you"? Whatever happened to pulling the chair out for a lady? When you order food, how about asking if the lady you just met is hungry and would like some? To set the hook—or show her that you are interested in knowing her (and not just knowing her body)—reveal to her the genuine side of you, not the side you want your "boys" to see. Be patient: don't be so quick to ask for her number or give her a business card. (By the way, when did handing out business cards become popular? She is not a client.) As a matter of fact, let her suggest to you how she'd like to communicate further. And even if she doesn't, still say, "It was a pleasure meeting you."

Panfish

Just like trout, the best hooks to use are #8 and #10. Just make sure these are the thin, long shank hooks. Remember that panfish have small mouths. Some fishermen use jigs to catch panfish. If this is your choice, use jigs that are 1/16 to 1/32 oz.

It's the same with these types of women. Panfish are young and need to mature. During that process, how they are treated has a great deal to do with whether they develop into something more. They can just stay as they are and become red snapper. In theory, though, these women can mature to become trout or catfish well before they hit the saltwater stage of their forties. The great thing is that we, as men, have a lot do to with how they can mature.

If you are using the same hooks you would use for the trout-like women, then the panfish you hook may turn out to be a trout, and so on. If you talk to her with dignity and respect, she will grow to only accept that type of treatment. If you talk to her offensively and vulgarly, she may continue to accept that type of treatment. Remember that not all panfish are the same, so you can catch them with different hooks. In my experience, it works well to treat them like trout. You will catch many and will always be able to return to that fishing hole. Who knows, one of them might even mature to be a bass.

Catfish

When you hook a catfish, you'd better be ready for a fight. The hook size will vary from a 1/0 to 6/0. With a small hook, you will not catch the big catfish; if you use a larger hook, you may not catch anything unless a big catfish comes along. When going specifically after catfish, you need to have the right hook, or you will go hungry. If you really want a catfish, go with the treble hook. It is stronger, and you will have a better chance of holding the catfish.

The Fisherman and the Catch

The hook needed to catch this woman has to be strong enough to hold her. A woman from the hood, the track, or your "Around the Way Girl" just won't stay on the hook if it's not strong enough. You have to show that you have some street in you, some swagger, if you're thinking about hooking one of these women. These ladies don't really care what you have...hell, if you show them all that you do have, they will take you for all you got. And you'll be sitting back saying, "What in the hell just happened?" Just like catfish, they will eat anything.

Timing is everything with these women. If a club says that ladies get in for free by a certain time, then go before that time comes, as most of the women in the club will be catfish. Remember that catfish are bottom feeders, and for these women this could mean that every dime counts, so going to the club before they have to pay is not a bad idea. I'm not saying these women are gold-diggers or cheap. I'm saying these women don't play, and if you get caught tripping, you will fall...and hard. Like catfish, these women are spirited and can have a real mean streak. They can be downright dangerous. But they are smart because they have had to grow up faster due to their environment. They make a nice catch if you can handle them.

Bass

Hooking a bass is more difficult than hooking most other fish. Bass are so savvy that they can snatch your bait off the hook before you know it's gone. Bass hooks come in many shapes and sizes. Many fishermen use the #1 hook or 1/0 and 2/0 hooks. I have even used a 5/0 hook for those ten-inch worms or lizards. These hooks come in a wide bend or L bend. I won't even go into the different kinds of jigs and lures used for bass fishing. Have you ever wondered why they only have Bass Pro Tournaments, and why most TV fishing shows cater to catching bass? It's because bass is the best!

The Fisherman and the Catch

In the same way, these women are the best. They are hard to hook but well worth the time, energy, and money. Ladies, please don't take "money" the wrong way. What I am saying is that a man will have to spend money on hooking you, but not buying you. Let me explain.

Men, to hook this lady, you have to be TIGHT. What is your physical presentation like?

- Is your hair cut? Do you have a nice fade? If you are bald, make sure you don't have a five o'clock shadow at 10 a.m., or that you are walking around with a cul-de-sac on your head. You know what I mean— bald in the middle with hair on the sides.

- How is your smile, are your teeth clean? Do you floss every night? (You may chuckle, but flossing is what protects the gums; it prevents gum disease, which causes bad breath. So go to the dentist every four to six months, and floss daily.

You will not catch a bass with bad breath.)

- When was the last time you had a manicure and a pedicure? Clean nails, filed and not bitten down, and soft feet tell a lady that you know how to fish and you put "money" into your hooks.

- Are you dressed well, pressed and together? I'm not saying you have to go out and spend two hundred dollars on a pair of jeans. But your jeans or pants need to be on your waist. If you are into wearing the size forty pants, and your waist is a thirty-four, stay with the catfish, panfish, and maybe some trout. Bass is not having it!

Presentation is what makes her want to get closer so you can set the hook. If you are looking to hook this lady in the club by 9 p.m. (you know, when ladies usually get in free), she won't be there unless she is with a private party. You see what I mean: "money" will be spent. Let me go on the record and say that you will need to have a good job to hook a bass. You will need to know how to socialize in an upper-class environment and how to dress for any event. You'll need to get used to having manicures and pedicures. With bass, it's all about time, energy, and money. After all, the bass is a keeper and is usually the one you want to spend the rest of your life with, so she is the one you need to exhaust your time, energy, and money toward.

So, we've talked about the rod, lines, hooks and reels you will need to catch the various kinds of fish. You need the fishing rod to hold the test line, in just the right strength to hold the fish, and you need the right kind of hook. Then you reel in your catch.

Fishing for women is no different. What you have going for you will determine the size of your fishing rod. Your presentation gives strength to your test line. Both your rod and line need to be strong enough to secure the catch. Then there is the hook. You will know when you have hooked her because you will see it in her eyes as she looks at you, hear it in her voice as she talks to you, and feel it in her touch as she caresses you. Here is a hint: if she looks at you and cuts her eyes or rolls her head, she talks at you and not to you, or she moves away when you try to touch her, don't even think about setting the hook. Just say "Have a nice day," reel in your line, check your bait, and find another fishing hole. You might even want to change rigs and go after a different kind of lady.

A friend told me he had a line that would work on every type of lady. I told him that I did as well: it's called *the truth*. Go out there and use all those made-up lines if you want to; you will mess around and catch nothing. Use your lines wisely, compliment when appropriate, say thank you if you are turned down and walk away saying, "Have a nice day," "Good evening," or something else equally pleasant.

Just remember that you are the fisherman, and how you set up your rig will determine what you catch.

Catch and Release

I never understood this concept. Catch and release is just that—you spend hours fishing, and when you catch a fish, you let it go. Is that not the craziest thing you ever heard? LET IT GO!?

It was always my unwritten rule that, if I caught a fish, I was going to keep it and eat it. As I journeyed through the different levels of being a fisherman (yes, there are levels based on experience), the concept of catching and releasing a fish became clearer. To one who has been through it, this concept makes sense. You know there are fish that are not quite big enough to keep. The different types of fish have legal sizes and/or lengths that are acceptable, and if you get caught with one that's under the limit, you can be fined.

There are catch-and-release lakes that are used primarily to get practice, touch up your skills, and see what rigs work best. Fishermen have an honor code, just as golfers do, to do what is right for the fish, for conservation, and for the sport of fishing.

This concept applies to women and young ladies. Men, just because you can catch her, doesn't mean you need to put her on a fish string and keep her there until you are ready to filet. I know that in Atlanta, for example, there are probably ten females to every one male. This means that the fishing holes are overstocked with women. We need to be responsible fishermen and just say no, or don't even cast your line in the water. Here are some situations to steer clear of.

First, about the legal size limit, all I'm going to say is this: it does not matter how nice the fish looks or how mature the fish is. Face it, seventeen will get you twenty. I said this to a friend of mine and he did not know what that meant, so I'll tell you. If you are of adult age and you mess with a lady who is a minor, you will go to prison for about twenty years.

Second, be mindful that women are not to be played; they are to be played with. They are not to be abused; they are to be loved (or made love to). So, if you have no interest in her, or if your interest in her is only for one thing—getting her into bed—then release that fish. Things may end quite badly. If you don't believe me, go watch *A Thin Line Between Love and Hate*, *Fatal Attraction*, *Enough*, or *Play Misty for Me*. If that doesn't change you, picture someone behaving that way with your daughter.

Remember Matthew 13:48: "When [the net] was full, the fishermen pulled it up on the shore. Then they sat down and collected the good fish in baskets but threw the bad away." Even if you catch them successfully, release the fish that are not right to keep.

That's a Keeper!

Fishermen often use the phrase "That's a keeper!" This means the fish they reel in is what they wanted to catch and has the minimum

The Fisherman and the Catch

required length and size to put on the stringer, take home, and filet. But, as fishermen, we don't always catch what we're after.

The term that counters a keeper is a throwback. Throwback fish are not the legal length or size to keep on your stringer or they are not what you came after. The process of throwing back small fish gives the fish time me to grow and mature. Sometimes a fisherman will throw back a fish because it just does not look good.

Just because the term is *throwback* doesn't mean that you literally throw the fish back into the water. I do not like the term, actually, because any real fisherman knows that you have to carefully take the hook out of the fish, gently lay the fish back in the water, and wait for it to swim away. A real fisherman knows that when you set the hook and reel in the fish—only to determine you will have to let it go—the fish can go into shock. To prevent the fish from dying, you have to gently let the fish back in the water. Well, this is true for some fish like trout, panfish, and bass. Catfish, however, are tough—just take them off the hook and drop them back in the water.

So, how does this relate to women? As I mentioned, different types of fish will strike at the same bait. Wherever you are, there will be women of different types. It is up to you to determine which are the keepers and which you will be releasing.

The first time I thought of a woman as being a keeper was September 26, 1992. That was the day I said, "I do." Since then, my wife has been everything from a friend to a foe. She has been supportive, and she has let me know when I was tripping. She has been my right arm, and I have wanted to give her my left foot. She has been my lover, and my hater. She has been my soul mate, and my roommate. But all along she has been and will always be my keeper.

You will never know whether you have a keeper unless you take time and find out her requirements, what she is receptive to, how she maintains certain aspects of her life, and whether she respects herself. Most people today date someone for less than a year and rush off to get married. Then they sit back and try to figure out what went wrong and why it isn't working. Well, let me tell you what went wrong: you did not know her and she did not know you!

To get a better handle on whether a woman is a keeper, ask yourself these questions. I call this the Keeper Test.

The Keeper Test

Easy Questions

1. Did you sleep with her on the first date?
2. Did she go down on you on the first date? Or within the first three dates?
3. Did you move in together within the first six months?

Easy Questions help you see if she is easy to give it up. Answering yes to these questions may indicate that she is using her body to get what she wants. She is not confident in her mind about keeping a man, so she will give it up just to hold on to him. Don't think for one moment that you were the first she gave it up to this easily. Remember, there are plenty of lines in the water.

Rush Questions

1. Did she ask you what your income was within the first five months (or limits on your credit cards)?
2. Did she tell her parents about you in the first seven dates?
3. Did she introduce you to her parents within the first seven dates?

Yes answers to *Rush Questions* suggest that she is rushing into a serious relationship. Any woman that rushes will forget or intentionally leave out some very important information. Her focus is on whether you will be able to take care of her, rather than looking at how she will work together with you so that you can take care of each other.

Seeing Others Questions

1. When you met the parents or the siblings, did they call you by someone else's name?
2. Does she talk about other males and say, "We're just friends"?
3. Does she get calls that she ends quickly, saying, "I can't talk now"?

Answers to these questions can help you figure out if she is seeing other men. It also can show that she has taken so many other men around the family, no one is special enough for the family to really remember. She is still disentangling from other fishermen's lines, or she is still in the water fighting. Whatever the case, she is not ready to commit, and her family knows it.

Respect Questions

1. Did you meet her children within the first five dates?
2. On the first date, did you pick her up at home? Did you go inside the house?
3. Have any of her friends ever flirted with you?
4. Have you been intimate with any of her friends or anyone in her family?
5. Has she asked you to pay any of her bills within the first two months?

Yes answers to *Respect Questions* can mean that she has no respect for herself or her children. She does not know you, so why is she taking you around her children? If her friends are flirting with you or you have slept with one of her friends/family members, then they don't even respect her. I learned in the Marine Corps that respect is not given—it's earned, and it begins with respecting yourself. Any woman who is lacking respect for herself cannot earn respect from others, even those she considers her loved ones.

The Fisherman and the Catch

Issue Questions

1. Is she estranged from her father?
2. Is she estranged from her mother?
3. Has she ever asked you for money, not telling you how it will be used?
4. Does she still talk to and hang out with her ex?

Issue Questions probe whether she has deep-rooted issues with neglect and being abandoned. Yes answers to these questions could also indicate that she disregards other people's feelings, at least yours. Being estranged from parents is a strong indication that she has issues. Who does not talk to their parents? If she does not get along with her parents, it is an indication of how she might treat her children, or yours. There could be some deep insecurity and trust issues here. Furthermore, if she asks you for money and will not tell you what it is for, then she is hiding something or does not trust you enough to tell you what is going on. And any woman that still hangs out with her ex is not ready to let him go.

Trust Questions

1. Has she ever come by your house unannounced?
2. Is she constantly showing that she is suspicious of you?
3. Have you ever left her in your home alone and found that something was out of place when you came back?
4. When you were at her house and the phone rang, did she let the machine answer it (or does she let her cell calls go to voicemail)?

Closely related to both *Seeing Others Questions* and *Issue Questions*, *Trust Questions* explore whether she can be trusted. The first sign that she is not trustworthy is that she does not trust you. If this is the case, she will spend most of the relationship turning your natural friendships with other females into accusations that you are sleeping around. The reason she shows up unannounced is to catch you. In her mind, you are already guilty; she just has not caught you. In most cases, she is behaving in this manner because she may have been with someone in the past to whom she gave her heart and that person abused her love or cheated on her. Now she is not trusting and assumes all men are the same. I hate to say this, but her heart has been damaged, and most likely she will run you off. Without trust, you have nothing.

If you answered yes to the majority of questions in these six categories, then she is not a keeper. Put her back in the water until she matures. You remember the old saying, "There are plenty of fish is the sea"? This saying is all about women. Don't be so quick to reel one in; there are plenty of them out there. Get to know them before you get serious with one because you may be dealing with her for the rest of your life.

So, how do you measure a throwback? Well, if you answered no to most or all of the Keeper Test questions, then she is not an obvious throwback. However, as I said before, I don't like the term throwback. And when referring to women, it's tricky because "One man's throwback is another man's keeper." It all depends on what you are fishing for. You may very well want to fight for a woman that someone else would quickly release.

Fishing Etiquette

Is there such a thing as fishing etiquette? There is, and you need to learn it. When I was shown how to fish, there were rules in fishing. There was an honor code amongst fishermen. There was respect, not only for other fishermen, but for the fish as well.

Here are some etiquette tips that you should learn. The first short list is how they apply to catching fish. The second list is how they apply to fishing for women.

Tips on Fishing Etiquette

1. **Don't pollute.** Don't leave your trash all over the area you are fishing, and don't put your trash in the water. If you smoke, don't throw your butts in the water. Maintain the area as if you were at home. (I take that back—some

of you need to work on cleaning your homes). The general rule is, if it's not a part of nature, don't make it a part of nature.

2. **Leave the noise at home.** Radios, portable TVs, or anything else that makes noise is going to make the fish nervous. They will feel the vibrations in the water and not come around.

3. **Respect the environment.** Don't make changes to an area to suit your needs. Leave the area as it was created.

4. **RESPECT THE FISH.** Treat the fish with respect. If you have to catch and release, do it with care. Make sure you take the hook out without ripping up the fish. Lay the fish in the water in your hands and let the fish swim away.

Is there any difference when dealing with women? I think not! All women deserve to be treated in a way where the following etiquette is applied.

Tips on Etiquette When Fishing for Women

1. Don't pollute.

A woman does not need your trash, your drama, your inability to keep a job.

If you are the one that stays at home (there is nothing wrong with you staying at home, if this is the agreement between you and your wife), then clean the house, do the laundry, fold the clothes, and have her dinner ready when she gets home from work. Hell, I sound like the Babyface song "Soon as I Get Home." But you get what I'm saying—don't pollute! When she comes home from a long day of work, the last thing she needs is to stand on her feet and cook, clean, or do the laundry. Give her an opportunity to relax, release, and revive herself, and you can help her even more by having the children's homework done, her bathwater drawn, and a glass of wine sitting on edge of the tub.

This also applies to the men that have jobs. Don't just expect to come home and have dinner on the table. She may have been at work all day just like you or had plenty to do if she was at home with the children. Take her out to eat to show her how much she is appreciated.

2. Leave the noise at home.

What makes women nervous? Well, if you are a yeller, meaning that every time something does not go your way or goes wrong (bills not being paid, lack of money to buy the wants, an untidy house, other family butting in), you yell at her, like it's ALL her fault. Or you talk at her, giving her orders like she serves under you in the military. Even worse, you get so frustrated and depressed that you raise your hand to her. If you do this, then reel in your line—you are NOT deserving of a fish. As a matter of fact, take your fishing pole and break it in half, and then turn in your fishing license. Your license has been revoked! And to my fellow fishermen I say, if you see someone out there hitting a woman, you have this Bassmaster's permission to whip his ---!

Furthermore, leave your "baby momma drama" at home. If you are not paying support for your child, taking care of your child, helping raise your child, you will have "baby momma drama." If it's not handled, you don't need to be starting a new relationship. The last thing any woman needs is to get approached by some other woman and her friends about an issue she has nothing to do with. This only occurs because men are not stepping up and taking on their responsibilities. This is an indication to women that you are not man enough to take care of and handle life issues. If any woman is confronted with this drama, she needs to snap the line and move on. If you indulge in this behavior, you are not a fisherman; you're a boy playing in the water.

3. Respect her environment.

Don't try to change her. Accept the way she looks. Why do men want their women to look like someone else? Why do women go out of their way and pay to change their look to please men?

> RESPECT = **R**ealize your **e**ntire beauty and **s**elf-esteem so that **p**eople will **e**ndure and see (**c**) your **t**rue beauty.

Just so you know, if you make a change to your body, that change should come from hard work, determination and motivation, not by going to the doctor or the store. This is the difference between a real woman and a woman trying to be real. What's that old saying? "Work with what your mama gave you!"

Men, my brothers—and I'm talking to all men as my brothers—don't you ever forget this: NO MEANS NO, AND STOP MEANS STOP. It does not matter if she is your wife. If you do anything past NO or STOP, that will get you fifteen to twenty. It will also get you a good friend named Leroy or Bubba. If you need more elaboration, you will go to jail and you will get about fifteen to twenty years, and you will have your salad tossed by a Leroy or a Bubba. But seriously, besides the threat of jail, she will not look at you the same way nor will she ever respect you again.

4. **Lastly, RESPECT HER.**

Respect her mind and her soul; she is a queen, God's gift to men. No matter who she is, she is a woman, a female, the same as your mother. She deserves respect even if she does not respect herself. I have seen the worst of women growing up, and I have respected every last one of them, just by being courteous to them. It does not take much to say, "Thank you, ma'am" or "Have a good day."

The Fisherman and the Catch

Genesis 2:21–22 states, "So the LORD God caused the man to fall into a deep sleep; and while he was sleeping, He took of the man's ribs and closed up the place with flesh. Then the LORD God made a woman from the rib He had taken out of the man, and He brought her to the man."

As I said, woman is God's gift to man, made from man. You respect her because, when you do, you are respecting yourself.

Crossing Lines

One of the biggest problems when fishing, especially when fishing from a boat, is crossing lines. This means that, as you cast your line, it crosses over another fisherman's line, thus causing friction. If either one of you gets a bite while the lines are crossed, it will tangle your lines. If this happens, you may have to pull out a knife (or the other fisherman will) and physically cut your line. To avoid this, one of you will have to move over and get to a position where your lines will not cross.

When it comes to women, you and I both have seen this plenty of times. Just recall going to a club and someone walking in with a nice fish (oops, I mean lady). You look at her and she smiles, only being nice, but you think she is nibbling at your bait. Now, you know she came in with someone, but what you do not know is whether they are couple, co-workers, family, or just friends. All you see is your line moving. As soon as the other fisherman leaves, you make your way to where she is sitting and begin to see if she will take your bait. No sooner than you sit down, here comes the other fisherman. Now, if they are a couple and depending what kind of fisherman he is, you may be in a lot of trouble. Remember, you crossed the line.

Crossing lines has caused many fights and worse. The best way to resolve crossing lines is to apologize, tell him he is a lucky guy, and buy them both a drink.

Crossing the line also applies when asking women for something too soon. This does not just mean asking for sex too quickly. It could mean her phone number, her name, or personal information about herself or her family. Men need to just slow down a little. You do not have to be so quick to get everything right away.

Chapter 7

I watched the movie *A Beautiful Mind*, starring Russell Crowe. He plays a man with a gifted mind who could calculate numbers, odds, and theories so easily and intricately that it appeared he was going crazy. In one scene of the movie, he and some of his classmates are in a bar. There is a beautiful lady looking at him, as all his friends are looking at her. So Russell's character calculates the odds and comes up with the conclusion that if he comes right to the point, he will get her. So his line was, "Let's skip the conversation and drinks and get right to the sex." Of course, she slapped the piss out of him. I have seen this, heard it, even done it, and in every situation it was not a good experience. Even when I got what I wanted, it did not last.

Fishing Holes

A fishing hole is your spot. It's the area of the water where you are fishing. It's the location you head to again and again. Fishermen do this because they know the terrain and they feel comfortable in that familiar place. They know which fish are there, what rig to use, and which bait will get bites. Every fisherman has such a spot somewhere, whether it is off a pier, off a dock, off the banks, in the coves, or near the shrubs. Wherever your spot may be, it's your fishing hole.

I did not realize this when I began fishing. All I did was look to see where others were catching fish, and I would get close enough to them where I could be in the same water while not violating their space or crossing lines. It was always amazing to me that I could be ten feet from them, casting in the same direction, and they were catching fish but I was not. That's when it hit me:

The Fisherman and the Catch

I needed to find my own fishing hole. So I did. Every time I went to the lakes, I would go to the same spot. If others were there, I would fish around until they left, and then I would move into my spot. You see, nobody stays all day. You catch your limit, and then you leave.

There are plenty of fishing holes to catch women; it all depends on what type of woman you want to catch and where you feel comfortable. There are clubs, bars, gyms, restaurants, your job, recreation facilities, parks, and shopping centers. The best fishing hole that I have seen is on Sunday at church. I say this because all types of women go to church. Don't be fooled—just because it's a church, not all the women are holy sanctified.

A large percentage of women going to church are single, they are going through something, they are getting over something, or they're looking for a good man. All of which means that a fisherman can cast his line and get a bite. I know that, at my church, I sit back and just watch, or I walk past certain brothers and say, "Looks like you got one on the hook" or "Don't let that one off the hook."

Chapter 8

They laugh about me noticing, but it's just so obvious that the brothers are there looking for a women. But there is nothing wrong with looking for a woman at church. What *is* wrong is going to church *only* to find women.

It got to be so bad, and so funny, that I named a certain location in the church "The Fishing Hole." I named this location the fishing hole because all the women have to walk right past it, and all the brothers stand either in front of it or right inside the doorway and get hugs from all the women. And that is a fishing hole, a place where you know the terrain and where you get bites.

OK, I'm going to stop here because you might get the wrong impression about my church... However, as people always say, "Can I keep it real?"

You would think I have a scripture for this, but I don't. I will say this, and I mean it: much RESPECT (Realize your entire beauty and self-esteem so that people will endure and see your true beauty) to the women at my church.

The Fisherman and the Catch

I have seen some great fishing holes in my lifetime. In Atlanta, Detroit, Las Vegas, Los Angeles, Orlando, San Antonio, San Diego, and even in Belize and Jamaica. No matter what city you are in or what country you go to, there will be great fishing holes. Just remember the fish and the women are all the same. They both are great catches!

Fish Stories

Fish Stories are exaggerations, stretches of the truth, or in some cases outright lies. These are the stories fishermen tell about how they hooked the big fish and, as they were reeling it in, the line snapped, or a seal got it, or they let it go because the fish had been in the water for a long time and it did not feel right keeping it.

I remember one time that I went fishing with my brother-in-law. I had always been told that my brother-in-law was a "sport fisherman." Before we went fishing, he told me we would catch a lot of fish. He said he would show me how to catch them, scale and clean them, and filet and cook them. Well, what I learned was that, when you are going fishing, don't tell anyone what you are going to do, because all he showed me that day was how to bait a hook! But he did also say that he approved of me marrying his sister.

The Fisherman and the Catch

You remember the fish story that begins, "I once caught a fish THIS BIG," while the fisherman opens his arms wide?

My father used to tell me, "If you lie on it, it's going to shrink and not grow." For a boy growing up, that was devastating to hear. Maybe to avoid that curse, I started early...and that's how I learned to spot lies early on.

You know back when you were in fifth or sixth grade, and all your friends were asking who was a virgin? Everyone would claim they were not. Of course, everyone was lying. Well, I was not lying. I had my first child at fifteen years old and had had sex starting years before that. That's a different story.

In high school, I remember guys would lie about the girls they had been with, and I knew it was a lie because of the way they told the story and the way they acted. I knew because I had already had a child and had been with women. I just knew they were not telling the truth. I used to hate how the girls would get labeled, when in fact they were still virgins.

Chapter 9

Know that lying about a lady makes you less than a man. Even if a story is true, there is no need to say what someone did to you, or what you did to them. I know that everyone knows someone he or she thinks can be trusted with the utmost secret. Just remember that the person you are telling also has someone else he or she trusts, and so on and so on. Before you know it, your secret is out, and the story has been embellished.

Telling stories about women will come back to haunt you, even if the story is true. It shows you have to talk about things to fit in or be accepted by your friends. It's also an indication that you have no respect for the feelings of others. I had a friend who used to brag on the women he'd been with, until one day one of those women came to me and asked, "What's up with your boy?" When I asked what she was talking about, she replied that he acted like he did not want to get with her. Needless to say, she had a different story than he did about the intimacy in their relationship—or lack thereof. I never let on to him that I knew he was not telling the truth, but I never again believed him about anything else he ever told me. What he lost was my respect. If you lie about women or to women, how can you be trusted? You cannot! The consequences in telling stories are that you lose people's trust and respect. What's that old saying we men used to say? "All I have in this world is my word, and I don't break it for anyone."

Bassmaster

A Bassmaster is the highest title one can hold as a fisherman. Achieving it means you have been in competition and you have caught the best fish to win the title. This title is similar to winning the Masters in golf or winning at Wimbledon in tennis. The concept is the same. Simply stated, you are the best in your sport. *You* are the best, as these sports are individual sports, not team sports.

Achieving the title of Bassmaster by far surpasses the title of fisherman in the realm of fishing for women as well. To be a Bassmaster, your ability to love, communicate, and relate to women must be the best. The way you carry yourself in public or when you are alone is to be admired and respected. Even the details in your appearance matter

The Fisherman and the Catch

Now, I don't know who made up the word "Metrosexual" and where this description of men came from. Basically, it's a term for heterosexual men who pay attention to the way they look and have good taste in things like decorating or dining. The term in itself has always been suspect to real men. Bassmaster is far from the stereotypical "Metrosexual." Bassmaster is the Man of Men. In Greek mythology, he would be Apollo. Bassmaster is the Billy Dee of *Lady Sings the Blues* and the Sean Connery of the James Bond series. Bassmaster is E. F. Hutton when other men ask for advice and the one that women ask to talk to their son to get him on the right path. Most of all, earning the title of Bassmaster is acknowledgement that you have skills in the oldest of sports: women. It's not self absorption, or having a "big head." It's the achievement one gets from experience and the recognition one gets from other fishermen. To be Bassmaster is a privilege to hold and an honor to maintain.

When my daughter approached me and stated she had a boyfriend, my first reaction was to lock her in her room. After thinking about it, I told her to go get the dictionary and tell me the definition of *boyfriend*. So, she went to her room and came back with the dictionary and looked it up. When she found the word, I told her to read it. She said, "A male friend, a frequent or regular male companion in a romantic or sexual relationship." So, I asked her, "Are you romantic with him?" She said she wasn't. I asked, "Are you having a sexual relationship with him?" She frowned and she said, "NO!" Then I said, "You do not have a boyfriend; you have a friend who is a boy."

After a few days, I began to think about when I was her age, and at that time I'd had my first child. So, I went into discussing this book with her and explained the types of fish in relation to the types of women. At certain points, I felt she understood, and then there were points when I was sure I lost her. After about a month, I talked to her some more, and she said she understood what I was saying. I did not really know, until she wrote this poem:

The Fisherman and the Catch

FISHING
by my loving daughter

There are many types of fish that live beneath the waves
Some swim in schools, but others live in caves
Some are long, some are thin
Some are wide and some just dig right in

As a fisherman approaches and comes into view
All the fish scatter 'cause what happens is nothing new
As he readies his line, with a clever disguise
He tries real hard to win his prize

However, there are many lures to use
He must choose the right one or the fish will refuse
He finds the lure, hooks it on, and throws it into the sea
But it's up to the fish whether to agree

The fish agrees but now the fisherman must decide
Either keep the fish or cast it aside
If he keeps the fish he won't throw it back
But if he doesn't, the fish will wait for another attack

So the fisherman will continue to fish until his prize is won
But until that day happens his fishing is never done

You see, my fifteen-year-old daughter got this!
Will you?

Notes

The Fisherman and the Catch

Notes

Author's biography

RIC D. HARRIS had a passion to harness his experiences so that others could learn from them. After relating his theory to friends and to young men in need of guidance, he finally wrote *The Fisherman and the Catch* to share the valuable insights with the rest of us.

Born in the Motor City (Detroit, Michigan), Ric always strived to accomplish what others stated he could not. Ric was raised by a strong single mother who taught him never to quit no matter what the cost; he was shown the streets by a hustler father to whom Ric attributes his own street smarts; and he learned to defend himself at an early age thanks to the care of an older brother. These three influences still impact him today. Add to that, the catalyst of joining the United States Marines Corps right out of high school, and you have a recipe for Ric's now successful life.

Ric is a loving husband, father, and Christian who often says, "I tithe, serve, and give back...God is still working on the rest."

CPSIA information can be obtained at www.ICGtesting.com
Printed in the USA
241423LV00004B/4/P